EDEXCEL
GCSE MATHS
HIGHER

T0352830

Steve Cavill
Geoff Gibb

EXAM PRACTICE BOOK

powered by MyMaths.co.uk

OXFORD
UNIVERSITY PRESS

Great Clarendon Street, Oxford, OX2 6DP, United Kingdom

Oxford University Press is a department of the University of Oxford.
It furthers the University's objective of excellence in research,
scholarship, and education by publishing worldwide. Oxford is a
registered trade mark of Oxford University Press in the UK and in
certain other countries

British Library Cataloguing in Publication Data
Data available

978-0-19-835154-2

10 9 8 7 6 5 4 3

Paper used in the production of this book is a natural, recyclable
product made from wood grown in sustainable forests.
The manufacturing process conforms to the environmental
regulations of the country of origin.

Printed in Great Britain by Ashford Print and Publishing Services,
Gosport

Acknowledgements
Cover image: Jakub Krechowicz/Shutterstock

Although we have made every effort to trace and contact all
copyright holders before publication this has not been possible in all
cases. If notified, the publisher will rectify any errors or omissions at
the earliest opportunity.

1

Calculations 1

1 An integer, G, is rounded to give the value 10 000.

  a Write down a possible value for G. **[1 mark]**

Answer _____

  b Find the greatest possible difference between values for G. **[3 marks]**

....

....

....

....

....

....

Answer _____

2 In this question the year is 2015 and you must use all four digits once only in your answer to part **b**.

Ali says 'I can make a calculation with the answer 10'.
He writes

  $10 - 5 \times 2 = 10$

and says

  10 take away 5 is 5

  5 times 2 is 10.

  a Explain why Ali is wrong and give the correct answer to the calculation. **[2 marks]**

....

....

....

  b Write two different calculations each with the answer 10. **[2 marks]**

....

....

....

Answer _____ and _____

3   Gemma adds two integers and the answer is 19.

She says 'The difference between my numbers is 5'.

What are Gemma's two numbers?

Show that your answer is correct.   **[2 marks]**

....

....

....

....

....

Answer _____ and _____

4   Airlines have these rules about the size of bags that can be carried on to a plane.

A bag must have   length < 56 cm   and

width < 45 cm   and

depth < 25 cm

Jenny's bag has a depth of 24 cm.

The area of the front of the case is 2200 cm^2.

Sean says 'You won't be able to carry that case on to a plane.'

Jenny thinks she will be able to.

Show that Sean and Jenny could both be correct.   **[5 marks]**

....

....

....

....

....

....

....

....

....

5 Decide whether each statement is *always* true, *sometimes* true or *never* true.

In each case, give an example to support your answer.

a A number P, correct to the nearest integer, is 5.

Another number Q, correct to 1 decimal place, is 5.0.

So $P \neq Q$. [2 marks]

The statement is _____ true.

Example ....

....

....

....

b G is an integer and $0 \leq H \leq 1$.

$\dfrac{G}{H} > G$ [2 marks]

The statement is _____ true.

Example ....

....

....

....

6 Julie has a scientific calculator. It automatically applies the mathematical order of operations (BIDMAS).

Johann's calculator came free with a comic. It does not do BIDMAS. It simply does each calculation in the order it is entered.

Julie and Johann have a sheet of calculations to do.

a The first calculation is $4 \times 2 + 3 \div \square = ?$

Johann's thumb was covering the last number. They both get the same answer.

What is their answer and what number was covered up? [2 marks]

....

....

....

....

....

Answer _____ and _____ was covered up.

b The next three calculations are

$6 + 8 \div 4 = ?$

$2 \times 3^2 = ?$

$3 \times 4 + 2 = ?$

Arrange these calculations by the *differences* between Johann's and Julie's answers.

Put the calculation with the largest difference first.

Show your working clearly. **[4 marks]**

....

....

....

....

....

....

....

....

....

Answer _____

2

Expressions

1   The shape of the Earth is an oblate spheroid.

The formula for its volume is

$$V = \frac{4}{3}\pi a^2 c$$

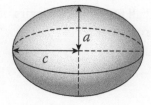

where

- *a* is the polar radius (distance between the centre and the North Pole)

- *c* is the equatorial radius (distance from the centre to the equator).

a   The internet gives the following information for the Earth.

Polar diameter (distance between N and S poles) = 7900 miles.
Equatorial diameter is 26 miles more.

Show that the volume of the earth is **approximately**
$2.6 \times 10^{11} = 260\ 000\ 000\ 000$ cubic miles.   **[4 marks]**

....

....

....

....

....

....

....

....

b   A silver ornament is made in the shape of an oblate spheroid with *a* = 3*c*.

Find an expression for its volume in terms of *c*.   **[3 marks]**

....

....

....

....

Answer _____

2   Here a is a whole number. You are given three facts about a rectangle:

- The length of the rectangle is a whole-number multiple of a.
- The width of the rectangle is a whole number.
- The area of the rectangle is $12a^2 + 6a$.

a   Find all **four** different pairs of expressions for the length and width of the rectangle.   **[4 marks]**

....

....

....

....

....

....

Answer _____

_____

b   An expression for the perimeter of the rectangle is $14a + k$.

Find the value of the integer k.   **[2 marks]**

....

....

....

....

....

....

Answer _____

3 Show that

$$\frac{8^{4x-1} \times 4^{x+4}}{2^{5+13x}} = 2^x$$

· ·

· ·

· ·

· ·

· ·

· ·

· ·

· ·

· ·

· ·

· ·

· ·

· ·

· ·

· ·

· ·

· ·

· ·

4 Lizzie drives a distance of $\frac{2}{3}p^2 + 2p$ miles at an average speed of $\frac{2p^2 + 8p}{3}$ mph.

Time = Distance ÷ Speed

a Show that this stage of her journey takes $\frac{p+3}{p+4}$ hours. **[3 marks]**

....

....

....

....

....

....

....

....

....

Lizzie stays at her destination for $\frac{5}{7(p+4)}$ hours.

b Show that the total time for the journey is $\frac{7p+a}{7p+b}$ hours, where a and b are integers.

Find the values of a and b. **[2 marks]**

....

....

....

....

....

....

....

....

....

$a = $ _____ $b = $ _____

Angles and polygons

1 The diagram is drawn using a square and two congruent rhombuses.

Shapes join full edge to full edge.

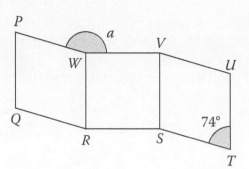

Not to scale

Bryn finds the value of *a*.

$\angle UTS = \angle WRQ = 74°$ Corresponding angles in rhombus

$\angle PWR = 180° - 74° = 116°$ Alternate angles between parallel lines

$\angle RWV = 90°$ Angles in a square

$\therefore a = 360° - 90° - 116° = 154°$ Angles in a quadrilateral add up to 360°

Bryn has made some mistakes.

Rewrite the working, correcting the errors and underlining the changes you make.   **[3 marks]**

....

....

....

....

2   **a**   This is a 1 cm square grid.

      Draw four more straight lines to create four congruent shapes that are not squares.

      Each line must start from the end of an existing line and finish on the perimeter
of the outer square.   **[2 marks]**

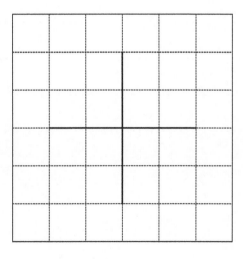

b What is the area of each congruent part? **[2 marks]**

....

....

....

....

....

Answer _____ cm^2

3 $AB = AD$ and $CB = CD$

BDE is a straight line.

Not to scale

Find the value of h, identifying any angles found in the process.

Give reasons for any two of the angles you find. **[6 marks]**

....

....

....

....

....

....

....

....

....

....

....

$h =$ _____

4 Two of these isosceles trapeziums are joined whole edge to whole edge to form a polygon.

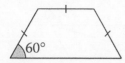

a Sketch all the polygons you can make from two of these trapeziums. [3 marks]

b Can any of these polygons be regular?
Explain your answer fully. [4 marks]

....

....

....

....

....

....

....

....

....

5 A parallelogram is defined as a quadrilateral with opposite sides parallel.

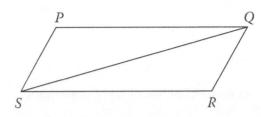

a Use this definition to prove that triangle *PQS* is congruent to triangle *RSQ*. **[3 marks]**

....

....

....

....

....

....

....

....

....

b What other properties of a parallelogram can you deduce from the result in part **a**? **[2 marks]**

....

....

....

....

....

....

4 # Handling data 1

1 Barry conducts a survey about the number of bedrooms people have in their homes.

He surveyed 20 people, each living in a different home.

The modal number of bedrooms was 3.

The smallest number of bedrooms was 1.

The range was 6.

The number of people living in 2-bedroomed homes was 1 less than the number living in homes with the modal number of bedrooms.

No one lived in a home with 5 bedrooms.

Use the axes to draw a possible bar chart to show Barry's results.

Label the axes.   **[7 marks]**

Number of bedrooms

....

....

....

....

....

2   All of these measures apply to a single set of five integers.

- Mode = 2
- Median = 2
- Mean = 3
- Range = 3

Find this set of five numbers.   **[3 marks]**

....

....

....

....

....

Answer _____

3   A set of five integers is given in numerical order as

   3   4 x 10 y

You are given that the upper quartile is 4 times the lower quartile and that the mean is also an integer.

Calculate all possible values of x and y.   **[5 marks]**

....

....

....

....

....

....

....

....

....

Answer _____

4 The children in two youth clubs can each choose to play one sport out of cricket, rounders or tennis.
   Their choices are shown in the pie chart and table below.

Club A

Sport	Frequency
Cricket	18
Rounders	12
Tennis	10

Club B

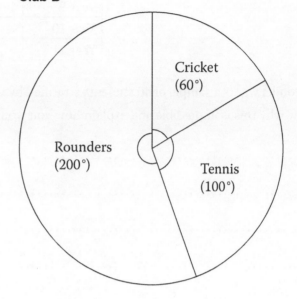

a Draw a pie chart to represent the number of children playing each sport in Club A. **[5 marks]**

....

....

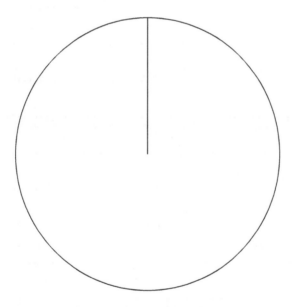

b i Saqib says 'Rounders is twice as popular as tennis in Club B.'
       Is he correct? Give a reason for your answer. **[2 marks]**

....

....

   ii Maria says 'There are more tennis players in Club B than Club A.'
       Is she correct? Explain your answer. **[2 marks]**

....

....

5   Weronika wants to conduct a survey on the amount of homework students in her school are given. The numbers of students in Years 9 to 11 are as follows.

Year 9	126
Year 10	101
Year 11	116

Weronika wants a sample of 40 students stratified by year group.

Show why this is impossible and explain how you would deal with this in real life.   **[5 marks]**

....

....

....

....

....

....

....

....

....

....

....

....

....

Answer _____

_____

_____

5

Fractions, decimals and percentages

1 Three shops each sell the same make of shirt for the same price.

Each shop has a sale.

Allan's
35% Off

TIP-TOP
Buy one get
the second
half price

Perry
$\frac{1}{3}$ off

Dan buys two shirts in one of the shops.

In which shop will he get the best deal?

Show how you decide. **[5 marks]**

....

....

....

....

....

....

....

....

2 Branka asked all the members of her year group if they preferred dogs to cats.

She found

- 0.6 preferred dogs
- $\frac{3}{10}$ did not prefer dogs
- 15% did not know.

Could Branka's results be correct? **[2 marks]**

....

....

....

....

....

3 Does the regular hexagon or the square have the greater fraction shaded?

The centre of each shape is marked with a dot.

Use fractions to show how you decide.

[5 marks]

....

....

....

....

....

....

....

....

....

....

....

....

....

....

....

4 40% of *g* is 8 more than 0.35 of *g*.

Find the value of *g*. **[4 marks]**

....

....

....

....

....

....

....

....

....

5 $\frac{1}{a}$ is a fraction where *a* is an integer between 1 and 10.

A number divided by this fraction is 50.

The same number multiplied by this fraction is 2.

What is the fraction? **[4 marks]**

....

....

....

....

....

....

....

....

....

6   Mikey divides two 2-digit numbers on his calculator. His display shows

What were his two numbers? Give *all* possible solutions.   **[5 marks]**

....

....

....

....

....

....

....

....

....

....

....

....

....

Formulae and functions

1   If a right-angled triangle has three sides whose lengths are whole numbers, then those three numbers are known as a Pythagorean triple. This question investigates ways of forming Pythagorean triples.

   a   Let $m = 2$ and $n = 1$. Calculate

   i $2mn$ **[1 mark]**

   ....

   Answer _____

   ii $m^2 - n^2$ **[1 mark]**

   ....

   Answer _____

   iii $m^2 + n^2$ **[1 mark]**

   ....

   Answer _____

   b   Show that your three answers in part **a** satisfy Pythagoras' theorem, $a^2 + b^2 = c^2$.   **[2 marks]**

   ....

   ....

   ....

   ....

   ....

The three expressions in part **a** generate a Pythagorean triple for all positive whole number values of m and n.

c Use $m = 3$ and $n = 2$ to generate a Pythagorean triple and show that it satisfies Pythagoras' theorem. **[4 marks]**

....

....

....

....

....

....

....

....

d Use the expressions from part **a** to generate a Pythagorean triple with one side as 33. **[3 marks]**

State your values of m and n clearly.

....

....

....

....

....

....

....

....

Pythagorean triple _____ $m =$ _____ $n =$ _____

e Show that a triangle with sides $2mn$, $m^2 - n^2$ and $m^2 + n^2$ satisfies Pythagoras' theorem. **[6 marks]**

....

....

....

....

....

....

....

....

....

2 The function f is defined as $f(x) = 3x - 2$ for all real numbers.

a Find

i $f\left(\frac{1}{3}\right)$ **[1 mark]**

....

....

....

Answer _____

ii $f\left(f\left(\frac{1}{3}\right)\right)$ **[1 mark]**

....

....

....

Answer _____

The function g is defined as $g(x) = \dfrac{f(x)}{f(3x-2)}$.

b Find and simplify an expression for $g^{-1}(x)$. **[5 marks]**

Answer _____

Working in 2D

1 The parallelogram and the triangle have the same area.

They also have the same height.

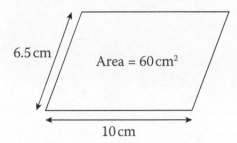 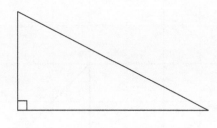

Find the length of the base of the triangle. **[4 marks]**

....

....

....

....

....

Length of triangle's base = _____ cm

2 The length, width and area of a rectangle are shown.

Each of the measurements is metric but no units are included.

```
┌─────────────────────────────┐
│                             │
│                             │
│       Area = 7.2            │  width = 1.2
│                             │
│                             │
└─────────────────────────────┘
         length = 60
```

Complete the statement by writing in the units used and show that your values
give the correct answer. **[4 marks]**

The length is 60 _____, the width is 1.2 _____ and the area is 7.2 _____.

....

....

....

3 A triangle and a square are drawn on a grid.

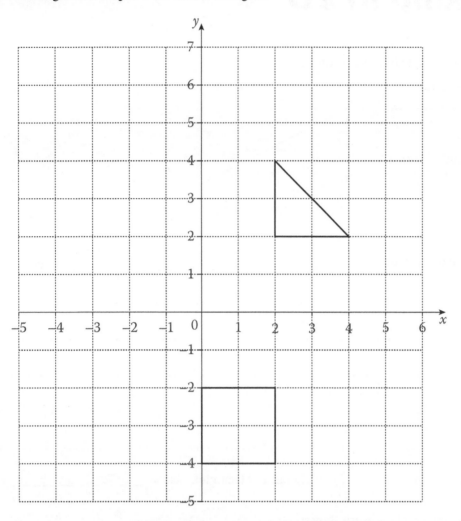

The triangle is transformed using a single transformation.

The square is also transformed using a single transformation.

The two images do not overlap and they form a trapezium.

The transformations used are a rotation and a reflection.

Draw the trapezium and describe the two transformations fully. **[4 marks]**

....

....

....

The _____ is reflected_____

....

....

....

The _____ is rotated_____

4 The line *AC* is the hypotenuse of a right-angled triangle, *ABC*.

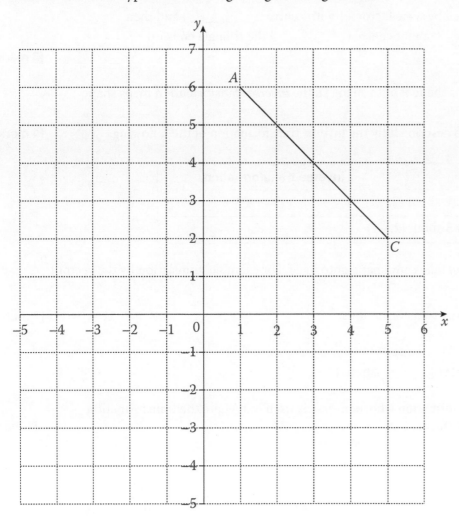

Triangle *ABC* is an enlargement of triangle *PQR* drawn using scale factor 2 and centre (−3, −2).

AC corresponds to *PQ*.

Write down the possible coordinates of *Q*. **[6 marks]**

....

....

....

....

(_____ , _____) and (_____ , _____)

5 Complete this sentence.

When a triangle is enlarged by scale factor −1 with centre (_____ , _____) and then rotated through _____ ° about centre (_____ , _____) the triangle ends up where it started.

[3 marks]

6 If a transformation **T** maps shape **P** onto shape **Q**, the *inverse* transformation maps shape **Q** onto shape **P**.

a Complete the table to describe fully the inverse transformation of the following.

[4 marks]

Transformation	Inverse transformation
Rotation 90° anticlockwise about (2, −1)	
Enlargement scale factor 3 about (2, −1)	

An *identity transformation* maps any shape onto itself. For example, translation by the vector $\begin{pmatrix} 0 \\ 0 \end{pmatrix}$.

b Complete these identity transformations.

[4 marks]

Enlargement scale factor _____ about (_____ , _____)

Rotation through angle _____ about (_____ , _____)

c Describe fully a transformation whose inverse is itself but where the transformation **is not** an identity transformation.

[1 mark]

....

....

....

....

8 Probability

1   Somebody claims that nobody in the world has a number of famiy members that is exactly equal to the average.

Explain why this is likely true.   **[2 marks]**

....

....

....

....

....

2   In this question, give each probability as a fraction in its simplest form.

A set of dominoes consists of 28 tiles numbered blank-blank, blank-1, blank-2, ... up to blank-6, then 1-1, 1-2, ... up to 1-6 and so on up to 6-6.

a   Jayne draws a domino at random from a full set.

Find the probability that

i   it contains at least one 4   **[2 marks]**

....

....

Answer _____

ii   its spots add up to at least 9.   **[3 marks]**

....

....

....

Answer _____

Fifteen of the dominoes have an even number of dots on them altogether (not counting the blank-blank domino).

b **i** Jayne draws a domino at random from a full set and sees that it is a 4-6. She does not return this domino to the set.

She now draws a second domino.

What is the probability that this domino has an even number of dots on it? **[2 marks]**

....

....

....

Answer _____

ii In a different experiment, Jayne draws a domino at random from a full set and records if it has an even number of dots on it. Then she returns the domino to the set. She does this 70 times.

How many times should she expect to get a domino with an even number of dots on it? **[3 marks]**

....

....

....

Answer _____

c Stanley says that the probability of drawing a domino at random from a full set and getting a domino with an odd number of dots on it must be $1 - \frac{15}{28} = \frac{13}{28}$.

Explain why Stanley is wrong. **[2 marks]**

....

....

....

....

3 Lianne has a fair, circular spinner with red, green, blue, yellow and black sectors.

There is a 15% chance of landing on red.

The probability of landing on green is $\frac{1}{4}$ and the probability of landing on blue is $\frac{3}{10}$.

The spinner is 100% more likely to land on black than yellow.

a Complete this table of sector angles used to make the spinner. **[6 marks]**

Colour	Sector angle
Red	
Green	
Blue	108°
Yellow	
Black	

....

....

....

....

....

....

....

....

....

....

....

....

....

....

....

b Explain why the spinner can be called fair when the probability of landing on each colour is different. **[1 mark]**

....

....

....

4 Lizzie and Sam are trying to decide if a coin is biased. They each flip the coin a number of times and record how many times it lands on heads or tails.

Here are their results.

	Number of heads	Number of tails
Lizzie	3	7
Sam	44	46

a Whose results will be more reliable? Why? **[1 mark]**

Answer _____

_____

b What is the relative frequency of heads? **[1 mark]**

....

....

....

Answer _____

c Is the coin biased? Give a reason for your answer **[1 mark]**

Answer _____

_____

9 Measures and accuracy

1 Lenny's car can carry a maximum total weight of 1174 pounds.

(This includes everything extra put in the car: people, fuel, etc.)

Lenny weighs 191 pounds and 1 litre of diesel weighs 0.85 kilograms.

Lenny has about 25 litres of diesel in the tank of his car.

He has to collect 985 bricks that each weigh between 2.5 and 2.7 kilograms.

A kilogram is roughly 2.2 pounds.

Use rounding to estimate the number of trips Lenny will need to make to safely collect all the bricks.   **[5 marks]**

....

....

....

....

....

....

....

....

....

....

....

....

....

Answer _____

2 The digits of the date 2015 are each used once in a calculation.

The symbols +, −, ×, ÷ and ( ) can be used.

Examples are $2 + 0 + 1 - 5$ and $50 - 21$.

Find five different calculations each with the answer 5.

Different calculations must have different symbols between numbers and not just a different order.

For example:

$2 + 0 + 1 - 5$ and $2 - 5 + 0 + 1$ are **not** different (same numbers and symbols reordered).

$2 + 0 + 1 - 5$ and $2 + 0 + 1 \times 5$ are different (-5 has changed to $\times 5$)   **[4 marks]**

....

....

....

....

....

Answer _____

_____

_____

_____

_____

3 A rectangle is four times as long as it is wide.

The perimeter is 80 cm correct to the nearest centimetre.

Calculate the minimum possible length of the rectangle.   **[3 marks]**

....

....

....

....

Answer _____ cm

4 The density of gold is 19.3 g/cm³.

The diameter of an Olympic medal is 60 mm.

Pure gold costs £24 000 for 1 kg.

302 gold medals were won at the 2012 Olympic Games in London.

By finding the cost of a layer of pure gold, 0.5 mm thick, on one face of one medal, estimate the cost of coating both faces of all the medals with gold.

> You may find this information helpful:
> Volume of a prism
> V = area of cross-section × length
> Area of a circle
> $A = \pi r^2$
> π is approximately 3.142

[8 marks]

....

....

....

....

....

....

....

....

....

....

....

....

....

....

....

....

....

....

£ _____

5   Richard wants to estimate the population density of Ghana, a country in West Africa.

The distance from Paga to Cape Coast is 800 km and the distance from Enchi to Lome is 600 km, correct to the nearest 100 km.

The population of Ghana is 26 million, correct to the nearest million.

Estimate the maximum population density of Ghana suggested by this data, by first approximating the shape of Ghana with a sensible two-dimensional shape.   **[5 marks]**

....

....

....

....

....

....

....

....

....

Answer _____

0 **Equations and inequalities**

1 Find the value of x in this triangle. **[3 marks]**

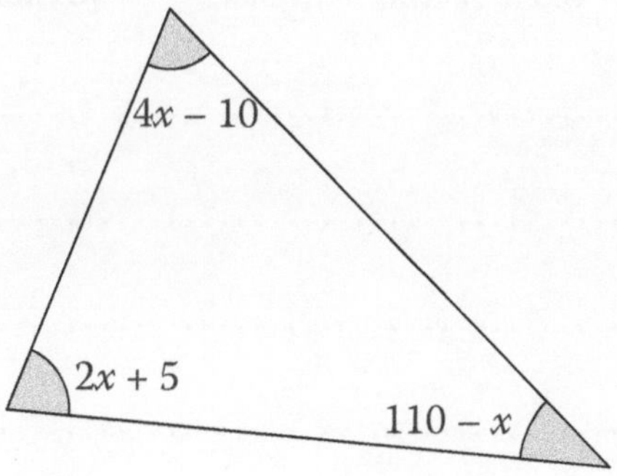

....

....

....

....

....

Answer _____

2 The area of this rectangle is $12\,cm^2$.

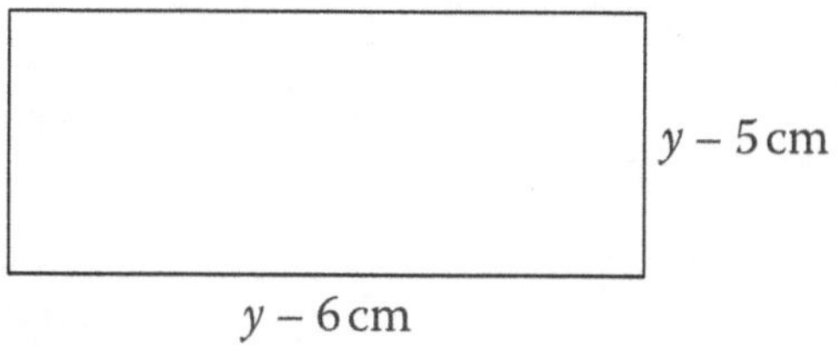

$y - 5\,cm$

$y - 6\,cm$

Use algebra to find the possible values of y and comment on your solutions. **[5 marks]**

....

....

....

....

....

Answer _____

_____

3 Sam collects 2 pence pieces and 5 pence pieces in a jar.

Altogether he has 157 coins and they are worth £5.90.

Let the number of 2 pence pieces be t and the number of 5 pence pieces be f.

Form and solve a pair of simultaneous equations to find how many of each coin Sam has. **[5 marks]**

....

....

....

....

....

....

....

....

....

Answer _____ 2p coins and _____ 5p coins

4 Here is Clinton's solution of the inequality $5 - 3x < 20$.

$5 - 3x < 20$

$\quad -3x < 25$

$\quad\quad x < -\dfrac{25}{3}$

He has made two errors.

Explain his errors. **[2 marks]**

....

....

....

....

Error 1 _____

Error 2 _____

5 This trapezium has an area of 114 cm².

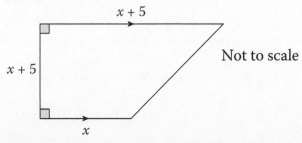

Not to scale

Show that the perimeter of the trapezium is 44 cm. **[7 marks]**

....

....

....

....

....

....

....

....

....

....

....

....

....

....

....

....

....

....

6   By writing $x^2 - 8x + 21$ in the form $(x \pm p)^2 + q$, find for which values of k
     $x^2 - 8x + 21 = k$ has real solutions.   **[3 marks]**

....

....

....

....

....

Answer _____

1 Circles and constructions

1 A silver decoration is made from two circles and a square.

The dots mark the centre of each circle.

The square has side length 6 cm and the decoration is 2 mm thick.

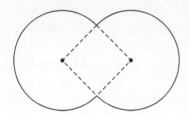

<table>
<tr><td>

Information

Silver costs 30p per gram.

$1 \, cm^3$ of silver has mass 10.5 g.

To find the volume of the decoration, multiply the area of the front face in cm^2 by the thickness in cm.

</td></tr>
</table>

Find the cost of the silver used to make the decoration.   **[7 marks]**

....

....

....

....

....

....

....

....

....

....

....

....

....

....

....

£ _____

2 The perimeter of a square is equal to the circumference of a circle with radius 10 cm.
Find the area of the square. **[3 marks]**

....

....

....

....

....

....

....

....

Answer _____ cm²

3 The diagram shows a rectangle *ABCD*, the bisector of angle *BAD* and an arc with centre *C*.

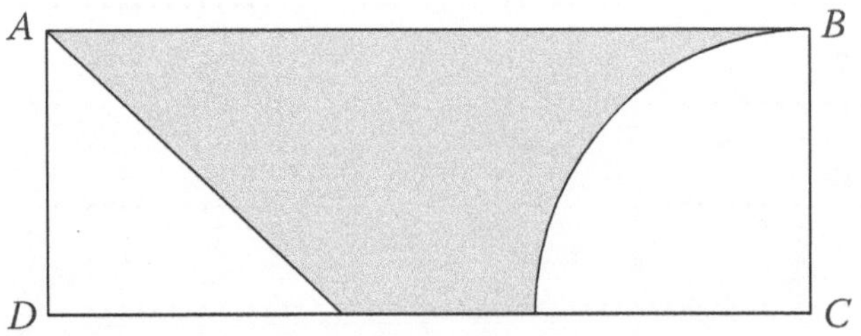

Complete this description of the shaded region. **[2 marks]**

The shaded region is the locus of points inside the rectangle that are _____

_____

_____

_____

4   Use only a pair of compasses, straight edge and pencil to answer this question.
Do not measure any lengths and do not rub out your arcs.

Draw a sketch to show a square with the midpoints of two adjacent sides joined.

Draw the shape accurately.

One side of the square has been drawn for you.

[6 marks]

5   *A*, *B* and *D* are points on a circle with centre *O*.

Angle *BAO* = 25° and angle *ABD* = 30°. *AD* = *AO* and *AC* = *DC*.

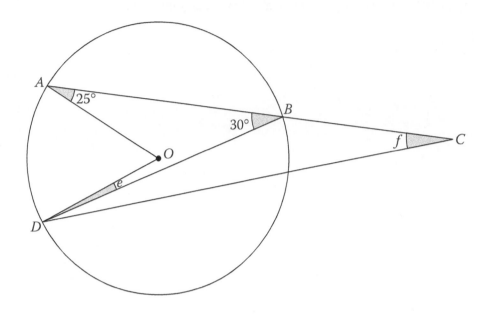

Find angles *BDO* and *ACD*, marked *e* and *f* respectively, giving reasons for your answer.   **[7 marks]**

....

....

....

....

....

....

....

....

....

....

Angle *BDO* = _____ and angle *ACD* = _____

2 Ratio and proportion

1   Dwayne and Julie work at the same factory. Dwayne earns £700 per month and Julie earns £800 per month.

Julie's boss gives her a pay rise of 16%.

Dwayne wants to earn the same as Julie.

Show that he can do that with a percentage pay rise that is roughly double that of Julie's.   **[5 marks]**

....

....

....

....

....

....

....

....

....

....

....

....

2 Grandpa Nick invests £20 000 in an account that pays 2% simple interest each year.

At the end of each year he divides the interest earned between his three grandchildren, Alice, Beth and Connor, in the ratio of their ages.

In the year 2010 he gave Connor, who had only recently started school, £250, and Beth was given twice as much as Alice.

a How old was Beth in 2010?   **[4 marks]**

Answer _____

One year Connor will get £32 more than Alice and £24 more than Beth.

b In what year will this happen?   **[5 marks]**

Answer _____

3   The map shows Hesk Fell in Cumbria. The scale is 1 : 25 000.

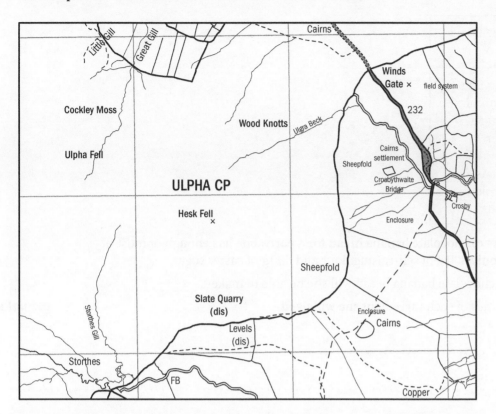

Alfred climbs Hesk Fell from Winds Gate. He marks his start and end points on the map with two crosses.

Alfred's route is the most direct possible.

Winds Gate is 232 metres above sea level. The vertical climb from Winds Gate to Hesk Fell is 250 metres.

Work out how far Alfred walks.

Show all your working and state any assumptions you have made.   **[5 marks]**

....

....

....

....

....

....

....

....

....

....

Answer _____

4   A recipe for chocolate banana bread contains these ingredients.

> Chocolate banana bread
> makes 12 slices
>
> 250 g self-raising flour
> A good pinch of salt
> 150 g caster sugar
> 100 g butter
> 2 eggs
> 2 large bananas
> 75 g dark chocolate
> 100 g walnuts

Jo wants to make lots of chocolate banana bread for a party. She has enough of most of the ingredients but only 800 g of self-raising flour and 500 g of caster sugar.

How many slices of chocolate banana bread will she be able to make?

Work out the quantities of each ingredient she will need.   **[5 marks]**

....

....

....

....

....

....

....

....

....

Answer _____ slices of bread

self-raising flour   _____

salt   _____

caster sugar   _____

butter   _____

eggs   _____

bananas   _____

dark chocolate   _____

walnuts   _____

3 | Factors, powers and roots

1 Here are two lists.

Each list contains two of the multiples of an integer between 1 and 10.

Multiples of X		66			84

Multiples of Y		80				112

Find the lowest common multiple (LCM) of the numbers X and Y. **[5 marks]**

....

....

....

....

....

....

....

Answer _____

2 Trains arrive at the station every 5 minutes starting from 10 a.m.

Buses from the town centre arrive at the station every 6 minutes from 10 a.m. onwards.

Don gets on a bus that arrives at the station between 10 a.m. and 11 a.m.

What is the probability that Don's bus arrives at the station at the same time as a train?

Show how you decide, justifying any decisions you make. **[5 marks]**

....

....

....

....

....

....

....

Answer _____

3 a Write 440 as the product of its prime factors.   **[2 marks]**

....

....

....

....

....

....

....

Answer _____

b Annie has a can that holds 440 ml of liquid.
She finds that she can use all the liquid to fill a cuboid.
The internal dimensions of the cuboid are all integers.
None of the dimensions is greater than 20 cm.
Find the dimensions of all the possible cuboids.

[5 marks]

....

....

....

....

....

....

....

....

Answer _____

4 **a** Write 100 as the product of its prime factors using indices. **[1 mark]**

....

....

Answer _____

b A googol is the name for the number represented as 1 followed by a hundred zeros.

Write a googol as the product of its prime factors using indices. **[2 marks]**

....

....

Answer _____

5 Solve $7\sqrt{8} - x = \sqrt{50}$, giving your answer as simply as possible. **[4 marks]**

....

....

....

....

....

....

....

....

....

....

Answer _____

6   The area of this triangle is 12 cm².

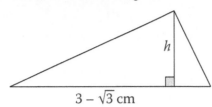

$3 - \sqrt{3}$ cm

Show that $h = 12 + 4\sqrt{3}$ cm.   **[5 marks]**

....

....

....

....

....

....

....

....

....

....

....

....

....

....

....

....

....

....

4 Graphs 1

1 Jacob takes the bus to school, and the bus-stops are a short distance from his house and from the school, respectively.

This sketch of a distance–time graph represents Jacob's journey to school one day.

Explain what each section of the graph represents, and give one way in which the graph does not represent the real-life situation.

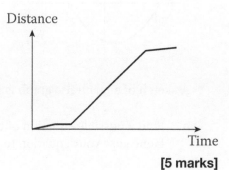

Distance

Time

[5 marks]

....

....

....

....

....

....

....

....

....

2 Line L has the equation $y = 4x - 7$.

a Which equation represents a line that is perpendicular to line L?   **[1 mark]**

   A $y = -4x + 2$ **B** $y = -\frac{1}{4}x + 2$ **C** $y = 4x + \frac{1}{7}$ **D** $y = \frac{1}{4}x + 7$

....

....

....

b Which equation represents a line that has the same y-intercept as line L?   **[1 mark]**

   A $y = -4x + 7$ **B** $y = 4$ **C** $2y = 7x - 14$ **D** $y = 4x + \frac{1}{7}$

....

....

....

3

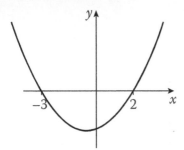

A sketch of a quadratic graph is given.

a   Find a possible equation of the graph, giving your answer in the form $y = ax^2 + bx + c$.
Hence use your equation to give the y-intercept of the graph.   **[4 marks]**

....

....

....

....

Equation _____ y-intercept _____

b

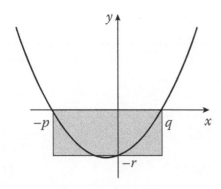

This quadratic graph has an equation of the form $y = x^2 + bx + c$.

It crosses the x-axis at $-p$ and q, and crosses the y-axis at $-r$.

The shaded rectangle has two adjacent vertices at $-p$ and q on the x-axis and its lower edge passes through $-r$ on the y-axis.

Find the area of the rectangle in terms of p and q.   **[3 marks]**

....

....

....

Answer _____

4   In 2009, Usain Bolt ran the 100 metres in a record-breaking 9.58 s.

One model for his velocity, y m/s, at time x s while he was accelerating is

$y = -0.4x^2 + 4.4x$.

When he reached his maximum velocity, he ran at this velocity for the rest of the 100 metres.

a   By completing the square, find the maximum value of $y = -0.4x^2 + 4.4x$ and the value of x at which it occurs.   **[6 marks]**

....

....

....

....

....

....

....

....

....

....

....

....

....

....

....

....

....

....

Maximum value _____ occurs at _____

b Sketch the graph of velocity y against time x, for $0 \leq x \leq 10$. **[3 marks]**

c Find the distance travelled by Usain Bolt when he was running at constant speed. **[2 marks]**

....

....

....

....

....

....

Answer _____

5 **Working in 3D**

1 A cube is cut from the corner of a cuboid.

Choose from the words

      increases   stays the same   decreases

to complete this statement.

The volume of the cuboid _____ and the surface area of the

cuboid _____ **[2 marks]**

2 A cube has a volume that is numerically the same as its surface area.
Find the length of one edge of the cube.
What can you say about the units of your answer? **[4 marks]**

....

....

....

....

....

....

....

....

....

                Length of edge_____

Comment about units _____

_____

3   This is the plan view of a solid.

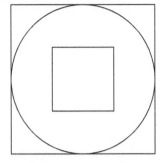

Use the grid and a ruler to draw two different side
elevations of the solid.

Hidden edges should be drawn as dotted.

(The two elevations must **not just** have different heights.)   **[4 marks]**

4 Milk is sold in packs that are square-based prisms.

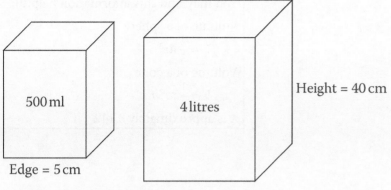

500 ml

Edge = 5 cm

4 litres

Height = 40 cm

Are the two packs mathematically similar?

Show how you decide.   **[8 marks]**

....

....

....

....

....

....

....

....

....

....

....

....

....

....

....

....

....

5   A bottle of roll-on deodorant is made up of a cylinder, a frustum of a cone and a hemisphere.

You may find this information helpful:

Volume of a sphere
$$V = \frac{4}{3}\pi r^3$$
Volume of a cone
$$V = \frac{1}{3}\pi r^2 h$$
π is approximately 3.142

Calculate the **exact** total volume of the bottle.   [10 marks]

....

....

....

....

....

....

....

....

....

....

....

....

....

....

....

....

....

Answer _____ cm^3

Handling data 2

1 This table summarises the ages of people living in a block of 8 flats.
No one in the flats is over 90 years old.

a Jenny works out an estimate of the mean age of these people.

Age (a, years)	Frequency
$0 < a \le 10$	3
$10 < a \le 20$	2
$20 < a \le 40$	5
$40 < a \le 60$	6
$60 < a \le 90$	4

$10 \times 3 = 30$ Total age $= 30 + 40 + 200 + 360 + 360$
$20 \times 2 = 40$ $= 990$
$40 \times 5 = 200$ Mean $= 990 \div 20 = 49.5$ years
$60 \times 6 = 360$
$90 \times 4 = 360$

Is Jenny's estimate of the mean age likely to be correct, too low or too high?

Explain your answer fully.   [2 marks]

Likely to be _____ because _____

_____

b Jenny drew this chart to show the data in her table.

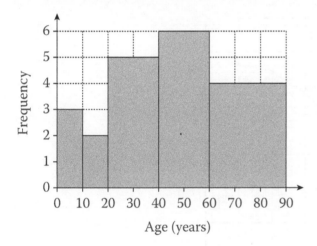

i Explain why this chart is misleading.   [2 marks]

_____

_____

_____

ii Use these axes to draw a better chart.

Remember to mark a scale on each axis and use as much of the grid as possible. **[4 marks]**

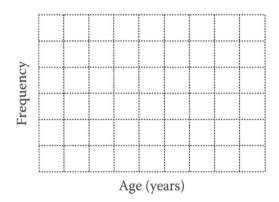

2 Amrit was given a new game.

He recorded his best score each week, but the score for week 9 was smudged.

Week	1	2	3	4	5	6	7	8	9	10
Score	50	70	68	74	78	68	78	84	⬛	88

The first eight results are shown on this time-series graph.

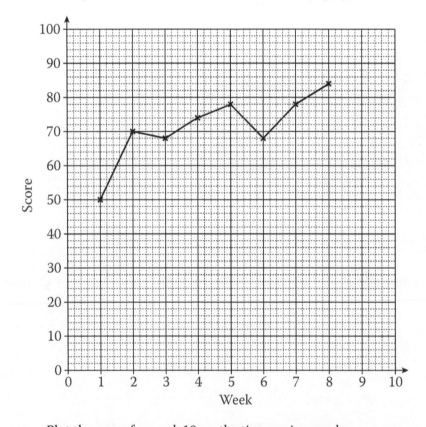

a Plot the score for week 10 on the time-series graph. **[1 mark]**

b Estimate Amrit's score for week 9 and explain, referring to the graph, why it may not be correct. **[2 marks]**

_____

_____

3 Three schools, J, K and L, recorded the GCSE Maths percentage for 100 of their students. They presented their results in different ways.

School J

Mark (m%)	Frequency
$0 < m \leq 10$	2
$10 < m \leq 20$	3
$20 < m \leq 30$	8
$30 < m \leq 40$	14
$40 < m \leq 50$	24
$50 < m \leq 60$	27
$60 < m \leq 70$	12
$70 < m \leq 80$	6
$80 < m \leq 90$	3
$90 < m \leq 100$	1

School K

Lowest mark	22
Range	48
Interquartile range	14
Median	52

We are very pleased that a quarter of our students scored at least 60%.

School L

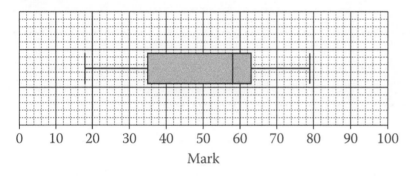

a Represent the results from School J on a cumulative frequency diagram. **[3 marks]**

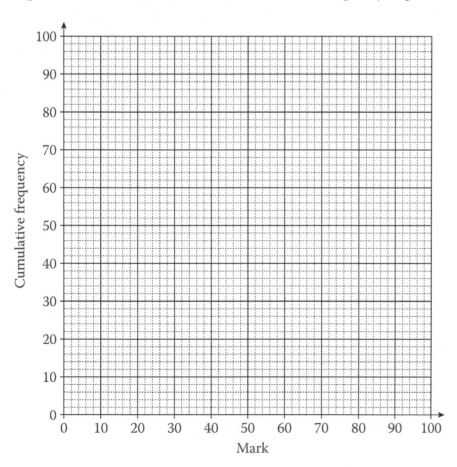

b Represent the results from School K on a box-and-whisker diagram. **[4 marks]**

Mark

c Write a report to outline the main differences between the results of the three schools. Support your conclusions with figures and give one concern you have about the validity of the data. **[5 marks]**

....

....

....

....

....

....

....

....

....

....

....

....

....

....

....

7 **Calculations 2**

1 A sphere has a surface area of π cm². For a sphere with surface area S, volume V and radius r: $V = \frac{4}{3}\pi r^3$ and $S = 4\pi r^2$. Work out the volume of the sphere. Leave your answer in terms of π.

[5 marks]

....

....

....

....

....

....

....

Answer _____ cm³

2 Here are two rectangles, A and B.

All measurements are in centimetres.

A

$\sqrt{k}$

B

$\sqrt{8}$

Not to scale

$\sqrt{10}$

$\sqrt{5}$

In each case below, find an integer value for k and show that it is correct.

Do not use a calculator.

[4 marks]

a The area of A is less than the area of B.

....

....

....

$k = $ _____

b The area of A is equal to the area of B.

....

....

....

$k = $ _____

3   There are roughly 6.41×10^7 people alive in the UK today.

Each person uses about 181 litres of water per day.

1 cubic metre = 10^3 litres.

Water costs approximately £2.34 per cubic metre.

Work out how much money is paid for water usage in the UK in a year.

Give your answer in pounds, correct to 3 significant figures and written in standard form.   **[3 marks]**

....

....

....

....

....

....

....

£ _____

4   A mixed fraction, expressed in its lowest terms, is in the form $a\dfrac{b}{c}$

The fraction is halved and then $\dfrac{3}{4}$ is added.

The result is $1\dfrac{9}{20}$.

Without using a calculator, and showing all your working, find the values of a, b and c.   **[5 marks]**

....

....

....

....

....

....

....

....

....

$a =$ _____ $b =$ _____ $c =$ _____

5 The ancient Greeks thought that a perfect rectangle had sides in the ratio $1 : \dfrac{1+\sqrt{5}}{2}$.

a Is this rectangle a perfect rectangle?
Show how you decide. **[3 marks]**

11 cm

6.5 cm

....

....

....

....

....

Answer _____

b The value $\dfrac{1+\sqrt{5}}{2}$ can be used to calculate a term in the Fibonacci sequence.

1, 1, 2, 3, 5, 8, . . .

The expression for the nth term is

$$\dfrac{\left(\dfrac{1+\sqrt{5}}{2}\right)^{n} - \left(1 - \left(\dfrac{1+\sqrt{5}}{2}\right)\right)^{n}}{\sqrt{5}}$$

Show that the formula gives the correct value for the 10th term in the Fibonacci sequence. **[3 marks]**

....

....

....

....

....

....

....

....

18 Graphs 2

1 **a** Complete this table of values for the function $y = x^3 - 3x + 1$. **[2 marks]**

....

....

....

x	−2	−1	0	1	2
y					3

b Draw the graph of $y = x^3 - 3x + 1$ for $-2 \le x \le 2$. **[2 marks]**

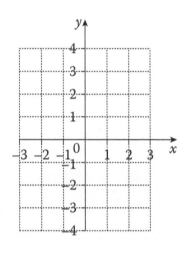

c Use your graph to solve $x^3 - 3x + 1 = 2$. **[2 marks]**

....

....

Answer _____

d Jess uses the graph to solve $x^3 - 3x + 1 = k$ for some value of k and finds that she has exactly two solutions.

Which two values of k could Jess have used? **[2 marks]**

....

....

Answer _____

2 **a** On the axes below sketch the graphs of $y = x^3$ and $y = \dfrac{1}{x}$. **[4 marks]**

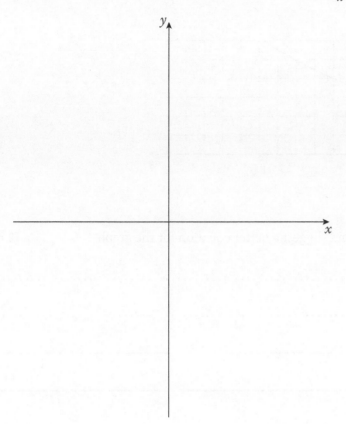

b By referring to your graphs, explain how many solutions the equation $x^3 = \dfrac{1}{x}$ has. **[2 marks]**

....

....

....

....

....

Answer _____

_____

3   a   Omar's teacher asks him to suggest the equation of this exponential graph.

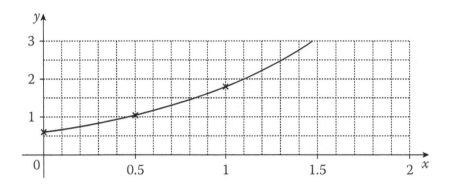

Omar says it is $y = 2^x$.

Explain how you know Omar is wrong and suggest a better equation for the graph.   **[2 marks]**

....

....

Answer _____

_____

b   Sketch the graphs of $y = 0.7 \times 2^x$ and $y = \dfrac{1}{x^2}$ for $0 \le x \le 3$ on the axes below.   **[3 marks]**

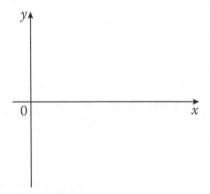

c   How many positive solutions will the equation $0.7 \times 2^x = \dfrac{1}{x^2}$ have?   **[1 mark]**

Answer _____

d   How many solutions altogether will the equation $0.7 \times 2^x = \dfrac{1}{x^2}$ have?   **[1 mark]**

Answer _____

4 Use algebra to find the coordinates of the point of intersection of the tangents to
$x^2 + y^2 = 25$ at the points $(0, 5)$ and $(4, 3)$.   **[9 marks]**

....

....

....

....

....

....

....

....

....

....

....

....

....

....

....

....

....

....

....

Answer _____

19 Pythagoras and trigonometry

1   Use calculations to decide whether or not this triangle is right-angled.

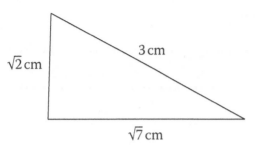

Not to scale

[3 marks]

....

....

....

....

Answer _____ because _____

2   In a game of racing cars, each car moves along vectors.

The diagram shows the first and last moves for one of the cars in a race.

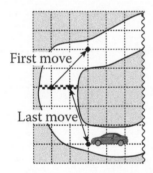

The vectors for all of the car's moves in the race are added together.

Write down the resultant.

Explain how you got your answer.

[3 marks]

Answer $\left(\quad\right)$ because_____

_____

3 The values for sines and cosines of angles from 0° to 360° are plotted on this graph.

Decide whether each statement is

- always true
- sometimes true
- never true.

Tick the correct box and show evidence when you think the statement is always true or sometimes true.

[4 marks]

a $\sin(x) = \cos(x)$

Always true	Sometimes true	Never true

....

....

b $\sin(x) > \cos(x)$

Always true	Sometimes true	Never true

....

....

4 Rosemary's herb garden is a triangle with sides 5 metres, 7 metres and 10 metres.
One afternoon she walks round and round the perimeter of the garden.

What is the largest angle she turns through? [4 marks]

....

....

....

....

....

....

....

Answer _____ °

5 Two rods, one of length 6 cm and the other of length 8 cm, are hinged at their centres.

The rods are rotated and the ends joined by straight lines to form a quadrilateral.

For example:

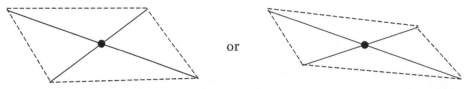

or

a Calculate the value of maximum perimeter – minimum perimeter. **[5 marks]**

....

....

....

....

....

....

....

....

....

....

....

....

Answer _____ cm

b Calculate the value of the smallest angle between the sides of the quadilateral when the rods are perpendicular to each other. **[3 marks]**

....

....

....

....

....

Answer _____ °

6

$\overrightarrow{OA} = 4\mathbf{a}$, $\overrightarrow{OB} = 4\mathbf{b}$. N divides AB in the ratio $3:1$. You are given that M, N and R are collinear, as are O, B and R. M is the midpoint of $\overrightarrow{OA}$.

Find $\overrightarrow{OR}$.

[8 marks]

....

....

....

....

....

....

....

....

....

....

....

....

....

....

....

....

Answer _____

20 Combined events

1 Choy asked some people which football team they supported.

The results are shown in the table.

Team	Arsenal	Liverpool	Chelsea	Bolton	Manchester United	Other clubs
Percentage of people supporting	15%	20%	18%	22%	17%	8%

Decide whether each statement is likely to be true and give a reason for your decision. **[4 marks]**

Choy says

a 'All the people I asked supported a football club.'

_____ because _____

_____

b 'The probability that a person from the UK, picked at random, is a Bolton supporter is 0.22.'

_____ because _____

_____

2 a On these Venn diagrams shade the areas that represent the given sets. **[2 marks]**

   i $A \cap B'$

   ii $A' \cup B'$

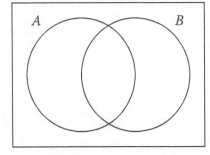

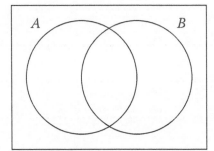

b If A and B are mutually exclusive events, what is $A \cap B$? **[1 mark]**

....

Answer_____

3 Three fair discs, each with the number 1 on one side and the number 2 on the other, are spun.

The three numbers showing are added together.

Gill says

'There are four possible totals'.

'You are equally likely to get any of the totals'.

'The probability of any of the totals is $\frac{1}{4}$'.

What errors has Gill made?

Show how you decide and give correct probabilities for each different total. **[6 marks]**

....

....

....

....

....

....

....

....

....

....

....

....

....

....

....

....

....

4   On 80% of the days when it rains, Joan gets a lift to school.

On 90% of the days when it is not raining, Joan walks to school.

Complete the tree diagram to show this situation.

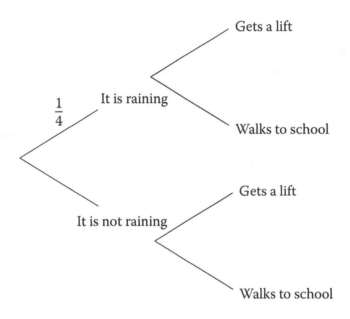

Joan goes to school on 200 days of the year.

On how many of these days can Joan expect to walk to school?   **[7 marks]**

....

....

....

....

....

....

....

....

....

....

....

....

Answer _____ days

5 Out of a year group of 200 students, 150 choose to play football, 120 choose to play rugby and 80 choose both.

Represent these values in an appropriate form and hence find the probability that a student chosen at random from this year group plays rugby given that they play football. **[5 marks]**

....

....

....

....

....

....

....

Answer _____

21 Sequences

1   Charlotte is making necklaces from black and white beads.

At each end she puts a black bead, and in between she puts groups of 3 white beads separated by another black bead.

For example:

This necklace has 4 black beads

and 9 white beads.

a   Sketch the necklace with 6 black beads.   **[1 mark]**

b   If Charlotte used 10 black beads to make a necklace

i   how many white beads would she use?   **[1 mark]**

....

Answer _____

ii   how many beads would she use altogether?   **[1 mark]**

....

Answer _____

c   Write an expression for the total number of beads Charlotte uses when she makes a necklace with n black beads.   **[2 marks]**

....

....

Answer _____

2 The Fibonacci sequence of numbers starts with 0, 1, and then each number is found by adding the two previous numbers.

It is common to label the Fibonacci numbers F_1, F_2, F_3, etc.

So $F_1 = 0$, $F_2 = 1$, $F_3 = 1$, $F_4 = 2$

a Write down F_5 and F_6 and work out F_{10}.   **[2 marks]**

....

....

$$F_5 = \text{_____} \quad F_6 = \text{_____} \quad F_{10} = \text{_____}$$

The Lucas sequence of numbers has the same rule as the Fibonacci numbers, but starting with 2, 1. They are given the labels L_1, L_2, L_3, etc.

b Complete this table showing the first 8 Lucas numbers.   **[2 marks]**

L_1	L_2	L_3	L_4	L_5	L_6	L_7	L_8
2	1	3	4				

c Write down the sequence of numbers formed by adding a Lucas number to the next-but-one Lucas number. For example, $L_1 + L_3 = 2 + 3 = 5$ **[2 marks]**

$L_1 + L_3$	5
$L_2 + L_4$	
$L_3 + L_5$	10
$L_4 + L_6$	
$L_5 + L_7$	
$L_6 + L_8$	

d Make a conjecture about what type of numbers are made by adding a Lucas number to the next-but-one Lucas number.   **[1 mark]**

Answer _____

_____

e Write a formula to show the connection between $L_n + L_{n+2}$ and F_n.   **[2 marks]**

....

....

....

Answer _____

f Investigate the sequence formed by $F_{n-2} + F_{n+2}$. **[3 marks]**

....

....

....

....

....

....

3 Trapezium numbers, T_n, are generated by diagrams like these.

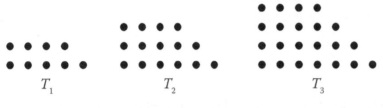

T_1 T_2 T_3

a Draw T_5 and write down how many dots it contains. **[2 marks]**

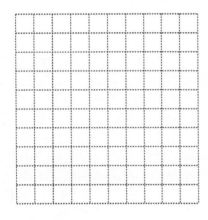

Number of dots _____

b How many dots are in the bottom row of T_n? **[1 mark]**

....

Answer _____

c Complete this table to show the number of dots in the first 5 trapezium numbers. **[2 marks]**

Trapezium number	Number of dots
T_1	
T_2	
T_3	
T_4	
T_5	

d Explain how you can tell from your table that trapezium numbers form a quadratic sequence. **[1 mark]**

....

....

....

....

e Find a formula for T_n. **[7 marks]**

....

....

....

....

....

....

....

....

....

....

....

....

....

....

....

....

Answer _____

22 Units and proportionality

1 The table below gives details, to 3 significant figures, on the population and area of some countries.

Country	Population (millions)	Area (miles²)
United Kingdom	62.0	94 100
Singapore	5.08	426
Mongolia	2.67	604 000
Bhutan	2.16	18 000

a Complete these sentences with the names of the appropriate countries.   **[2 marks]**

The population of .... is about 12 times the population of ....

The area of .... is about 5 times the area of ....

b Put the four countries in order of population density, from highest to lowest.
Show your working and make the units clear.   **[4 marks]**

....

....

....

....

....

....

....

....

....

....

Answer _____

_____

2 A pint glass is 15 cm tall.

A half-pint glass is mathematically similar and has half the capacity.

Calculate the height of the half-pint glass. **[4 marks]**

....

....

....

....

....

Answer _____ cm

3 In an electric circuit with constant potential difference, the current, I amperes, is inversely proportional to the resistance, R ohms.

When the resistance is 3 ohms, the current is 8 amperes.

a Find an equation connecting I and R. **[3 marks]**

....

....

....

....

....

....

Answer _____

b Find the **exact** value of R when I equals R. **[3 marks]**

....

....

....

....

....

Answer _____ ohms

4   A motoring website gives this information about the price of second-hand cars.

> A new car loses
>   • 40% of its value in its first year
>   • a further 20% of its value for each year after the first year

a   Geoff buys a new car for £15 000.

   i   How much is Geoff's car worth after one year?   [2 marks]

   ....

   ....

   £ _____

   ii   How much is Geoff's car worth after four years?   [3 marks]

   ....

   ....

   ....

   £ _____

   iii   Write an expression to show how much Geoff's car is worth after n years.   [2 marks]

   ....

   ....

   £ _____

b   The graph below shows the value of Geoff's car at the end of each year for the first 6 years.

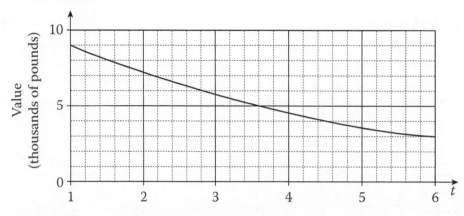

   Use the graph to find the average depreciation per year from the first year to the
   sixth year.   [2 marks]

   ....

   ....

   Answer _____